Stand Out, Get Into A Dream School

Stand Out, Get Into A Dream School

Seven Steps to Help Your Child Get into a Top College

© 2020 Rachel Collins

Published in New York, New York, by Morgan James Publishing. Morgan James is a trademark of Morgan James, LLC.
www.MorganJamesPublishing.com

ISBN 978-1-64279-625-4 paperback
ISBN 978-1-64279-626-1 eBook
Library of Congress Control Number: 2019907440

Cover Design by:
Rachel Lopez
www.r2cdesign.com

Interior Design by:
Bonnie Bushman
The Whole Caboodle Graphic Design

Morgan James is a proud partner of Habitat for Humanity Peninsula and Greater Williamsburg. Partners in building since 2006.

Get involved today! Visit
www.MorganJamesBuilds.com

Stand
OUT
GET INTO A
Dream
School

Seven Steps to Help Your Child
Get into a Top College

Rachel Collins

NEW YORK

LONDON • NASHVILLE • MELBOURNE • VANCOUVER

Table of Contents

One Ivy League Parent's Experience

We continue to thank our dear friend who recommended Rachel and College Prep Consulting. We believe Rachel's team is the reason Jonathan got into his dream school, Columbia University in New York.

Jonathan had ambitious hopes. But when it came to helping him figure out how to get into these competitive schools, we were drawing a blank. And without a philanthropic legacy nor a strong record of documented altruism, we knew that top schools might be out of reach.

We had heard horror stories from other families at his school. While he was at summer camp, she helped him come up with the idea of a developing a beekeeping workshop. When he came home, I remember he asked if that would be enough to get him into Columbia. Rachel simply stated that it wouldn't be.

She helped him understand that he would need to stand out. Her team helped him to brainstorm to do something further to develop evidence of his passion and helped him write about this passion. How amazing is that!

Through a series of brainstorming sessions with Rachel's team, Jonathan designed a project that stunned all of us. Over the course of two months we were amazed to watch him further deepen his passion and perform a small-scale experiment in our shed. After a great deal of online research into current studies on bees, and after a series of false starts, they landed on a project that turned out to be exactly perfect for him.

He went to the hardware store and bought a purple light. Before we knew it, he was conducting an experiment in our shed with a few of his bees and this purple light. We had not yet witnessed our son take such determined action outside the confines of his school and church, so we were amazed.

He had come up with the idea after weeks of being gently pushed by Rachel's team and there he was...our son, the scientist, creating actual data and writing up his findings.

As he moved forward on this project, he was simultaneously writing his college essays. Through continuing brainstorming sessions with Rachel's team, he created a main essay on this project that we considered miraculous. His mentors at College Prep Consulting had been pushing for a series of intellectual writings. And there they were.

These same mentors helped him create a video montage of himself in a variety of theater performances, and they decided which majors would increase his chances at each different school following an algorithm that Rachel designed. Each strategy was brilliant.

But the funny thing was. He got accepted to Columbia early decision, so we didn't get to see which other Ivy League schools would have taken him since he got accepted before Christmas. We've been celebrating ever since!

I suppose this is a good time and place to once again thank College Prep Consulting.

—**Eileen Fisher**, mom to
Jonathan, class of 2022

Introduction

The WOW factor to college admissions sprung from a series of meetings at Stanford. As I conversed with my fellow admissions department colleagues from Harvard, Columbia, and Yale, we realized that a distinctive pattern was emerging. While I had already spent many years as an admissions representative at Berkeley and Stanford, I was getting to the bottom of exactly what was getting students accepted at schools across the Ivy League.

After speaking with my colleagues, I engaged in a large-scale independent research experiment and began to analyze a series of meta-studies that are available through both online and periodical resources.

In response to these remarkable findings, I formed College Prep Consulting, Inc.

We are a team of seasoned professionals who share our knowledge and experience. Together with each student, we craft a plan suited for individual success. We are located in Northern California and are proud to assist clients throughout the United States.

In this book, I will share with you some of the practices that we have developed. Whatever amount of time your child has remaining before submission deadlines, he or she can engage in a process that will increase the odds of acceptance by at least 30%—and that 30% can make the difference in landing a spot.

In the years that my group has led hundreds of students through this process, it has become abundantly clear that this type of engagement is the one key factor that leads to dream school acceptances.

It is this combination of excellence positioning and intellectual essays that I truly believe is responsible for my group's success. Our students are successful because they are motivated to achieve their goals and willing to entrust their future with us, their mentors. As they discuss their future with us, they understand the importance of the endeavor.

Throughout my interviews with deans of admissions, two themes became clear: the primary elements that must be exhibited if a student is to be admitted to any of these schools is *singularity of focus* and *passion*. Unfortunately, most students have no idea how to venture out of their school in order to locate and develop this element. And not all of us have been playing the oboe since the age of three.

I am a true believer in transparency and access for all. I believe that admissions departments have a responsibility to make their institutions accessible for the sake of equity. Yet, in order to achieve this level of transparency, someone must lay out the laws in a way that all students can understand and use to their advantage. I consider this my personal mission.

Your child can use insider knowledge from Stanford, Harvard, Yale, Cornell, and Princeton to stand out and create what I call the WOW factor.

Chapter One

How to Get into a Top School

What makes your child stand out over all the others in the applicant pool? Why should schools admit your child over all of the others with the same or better grades and test scores?

Creative Action

Admissions teams want to see that your child has already proven herself as an impact maker with the gifts of initiative, intellect, and creativity. They want her because she has established herself in some small way as a person who takes creative action. Most importantly, she reflects deeply about her experience and creates powerful essays that hook the readers at any school.

Colleges have a long tradition of recruiting students for their athletic talent. Schools have always wanted strong sports teams to make a name for the school. Yet, people don't speak openly about the other type of recruiting. There isn't really even a name for it yet—I'll call it recruiting for *impact*.

Ivy League and top-tier schools across the United States are not specifically going out across the country to locate and recruit students who show evidence that they have impacted their community. But if you're a savvy parent, you can help your child take advantage of a strategy that I've developed that helps her reveal ways that she has impacted the community and will likely go on to impact her college community.

Many parents don't realize that schools seek candidates who will make a difference on their campus and in the world—not simply achieve high grades. There is an obvious left-brain element at play in the decision-making process. When students are discussed at the committee level in any school, there is naturally an emotional response to each applicant. In the same way that people make purchases emotionally and then justify their purchases logically, college committees select students emotionally and then rationalize their decisions logically.

Having read, analyzed, and scored thousands of applications for UC Berkeley and Stanford and having interviewed admissions professionals from Harvard, Yale, Penn, Columbia, and Princeton, I'm here to tell you that schools are no longer seeking what used to be known as the renaissance candidate (also known as the well-rounded kid who does some of everything).

While many students are not aiming for the top schools in the country, most students are aiming for the best school they can get into. The strategies and techniques that I have developed apply to any student applying to any mid- to top-tier school.

This book is my attempt to create some degree of transparency between our country's most selective admissions departments and your child. It is also my attempt to shed light on how students can engage in a process that results in much more powerful essays and applications. The goal is the creation of essays that hold the power to raise admissions teams up out of their seats as they recognize the unique activities and writings of your child and admit him or her over other students.

Future Change-Makers

Harvard, Yale, Princeton, Cornell, Brown, Columbia, and Penn want to see evidence that the candidate in question has the potential to impact the school, the community, and even quite possibly, down the road, the world.

But all these schools will happily settle for a glimmer of evidence that this candidate, who has risen through the ranks of the admissions process, will do something that might one day have an impact. Schools are now competing for *future change-makers*.

Impact can be built by a number of factors, each of which reflects a valuable component of an effective positioning plan. From the perspective of the admissions teams, impact and excellence are interchangeable. This type of creativity and ingenuity is the only real evidence to schools that a student will positively impact the school and the community.

We attempted to measure the importance of this pivot toward what Stanford calls the point of excellence (Harvard calls it the spark, Columbia named it intensity of purpose). Pondering this question over late-night lattes, we created a spreadsheet to capture this dramatic shift away from renaissance candidate to impact candidate.

One of my associates was staring at a blinking cursor at the top of the second column of an Excel spreadsheet. She stood up to show us the arc shown by the change in one single data point over time that represented what we came to see as a clear and obvious shift from an emphasis on simple grades, scores, and activities to a clear element of impact.

One key element in the creation of this point of excellence is that it is almost always a project that is designed and developed outside the confines of school.

It's easy to take small, independent steps toward one's passion. Even a few tiny yet creative and strategic steps can make a world of difference. Then, when it comes time to write the essays that are the true linchpin to hooking the committee, the essays practically write themselves.

Parent Experience

We started with Rachel five years ago with our older son, Jackson. His grades had been good, but he had a single-minded obsession with UCLA. Happily, he worked long and hard on his essays with Rachel and her colleague, and he got in. We waited until we couldn't wait anymore and introduced our second son, Brad, to Rachel when he was a sophomore.

He was aiming for the Ivy League, and we knew his chance lay with an early start. Brad was excited because he knew our older boy had such a great experience, and he had been hearing about Rachel for several years. Naturally, his conversations with Rachel and her group showed great promise. Through brainstorming, he became increasingly motivated. He not only volunteered with the library after his sophomore year, but Rachel encouraged him to begin to lead events, and together they came up with the idea for him to promote a lecture series at the library.

The library director, Angie, was amazed to have such a young student come in with such specific ideas. She became a secondary mentor through the summer. The lecture series was a big hit, and he entered junior year with a drive we had not seen in him before.

Junior year, his consultant at College Prep Consulting helped him to plan a campaign to run for student body president. It took every ounce of his focus, but he won!

We were impressed with the relationship he was developing with Rachel and her team, and we were relieved to step away completely. Over the summer, he brainstormed with the team and began work on a documentary about what he calls the modern library movement. Each week he worked with Rachel, and eventually he figured out exactly what he could do to forward his presidency, his documentary and his essays.

College Prep sent emails to him and to us with recaps and to-do lists that were so detailed, we were simply floored. We all chatted at the dinner table each night and tried to find ways to support him, but he seemed to know exactly what he was doing every day.

At another point in the summer, Rachel learned more about his passion for art and helped him to develop a website and blog on art. Soon after, however, he seemed overwhelmed. They helped him to realize that he was overextending himself. He agreed and found ways to prioritize himself and finish in time for the start of school.

Now he was a full-blown senior. Rachel helped him vet his final school list, prep for interviews, finalize his main essays, and keep his main priority focused on grades and test scores. They worked closely to determine majors and strategies for each of his top schools, and we were impressed at how "high-end" the email correspondence continued to be.

To our pleasant surprise, he was admitted restrictive early admission to Yale. This school is not for everyone, but it does seem to be the right way to go for him. He's starting there in the fall.

We are happy to speak with anyone who might want to learn about how College Prep can help their child. Please don't hesitate to get our phone number from Rachel. Our boys are both so happy, and we hope to share our incredible find.

—The Smith Family, Mill Valley

Chapter Two
Successful Essays

Essays are considered the one true element of the application that is completely within a student's control. This is partly true, and since they are within one's control, our students work long and hard to get them right.

The most successful essays are those that reveal deep curiosity and academic drive beyond the hard numbers of grades and test scores. But the larger question is how to find the strongest and most impactful content for the essays.

Unless your child is destined to be an English major, the best results will be achieved through content, not style.

Content is key. And the best content by far is that which revolves around each student's passion. In the shockingly quick turnaround time of a few months, your sixteen- or seventeen-year-old will take steps in the direction of their passions, reflect deeply on their process, and create multiple successful essays.

Happily, the thinking and the writing dovetail as your child reflects and writes her way through a handful of powerful essays that cause schools to click the Admit button. We regularly see schools respond with letters from deans of admissions that claim the essays clinched the offer of acceptance. The essays are the most human element, and we regularly see schools offer to meet whatever financial gap there is to get a student to attend.

Mentors can work efficiently to lead students through the early stage to land quickly on their strongest point of entry. The trick is to find a way to delve deeply into that specialty. Mentors should provide weekly to-do lists that help students dig deep and write deep. By the time students bring together their main essays, their content is rife with intelligent thinking and personal storytelling at its best.

While we now know that decisions are based on right-brain emotional response, we also know that those decisions are almost always backed up by left-brain *justification*. Being fully aware of this phenomenon, we have developed techniques to help students pepper their stories and statements with statistics, studies, and facts.

This type of deliberate academic writing serves multiple purposes. We know that schools seek students who enjoy deep thinking.

Committees want to know they are admitting individuals who are curious and intellectually driven. A student's second purpose should be to show (not tell) college committees how the student is truly a specialist.

It's difficult to quantify the long-term effects of this type of deep thinking and collaborative journey. But we do know that students continue to use the skills learned during our process well into their careers.

It's well known that there's no room on any application to dawdle. Each piece a student creates should show how he or she will impact the school's culture. Students create sequences of content, strategically linked from one topic to the next, to stimulate the readers and committee members as they are able to engage more fully. The more engaged the audience is in the content, the more likely they will become fans.

We have found that the gelling process surrounding point of excellence positioning, school selection, strategy, and especially essay writing takes as long as you've got.

To develop the point of excellence, a student must know her topics well and be able to translate them into powerful language. We're looking for ways that each essay will resonate with her audience and drive that audience to take action on her behalf.

This ability to resonate can come in multiple forms and in multiple essays. Most important of all is the main essay—also known as the calling card. But there are also short essays about various topics, school-specific writings and off-the-wall prompts, designed to weed out kids who don't want to do the work. The focus from the start should be on creating rich, intelligent content that constantly conveys reasons to help advocates argue for the student through heated committee discussions.

Very few of our students encounter writer's block, nor are they dogged by procrastination. Instead, we begin with rough scribbling and idea generation. Spider diagrams are our best friend through the early stages. I remind them that we can fix anything in the editing phase. Even then, unless the student is applying to be an English major, the writing doesn't need to be flawless. It's *all* about deep thinking and content.

Content

It is the mentor's job to help each student figure out a thesis statement that will allow the student to include research statistics, facts, and figures. Committees will be impressed, and his chances increase by at least 15% for each essay that is driven by passion and academic thinking.

The strongest candidates are those who have created a clear way for themselves to stand out. Once this standout position has been determined, the essays come naturally. Take Jaime, who planned to major in engineering. In the seven months before submission deadlines, he worked closely with us. Over a series of brainstorming sessions with me and my team, he was able to figure out a way to create a small-scale, unofficial "nonprofit." Jaime remembered that his church had sent a team of volunteers to build houses in Malaysia.

By his third session, Jaime had researched which types of seeds were growing most successfully in this particular climate, and he was able to work with a priest to send the appropriate seeds to a small group of Malaysian farmers.

As a side note, my partner and Jaime dug for information related to the highest popularity majors at his dream schools. Together, they figured out that he would have a better chance of acceptance by switching his first-choice major from engineering to the humanities. He simply did not have enough engineering experience to land a spot in a selective engineering department.

Jaime's father was vehemently opposed. He wanted his son to major in engineering or nothing. I helped him to better understand how the system works, and in the end, he decided to follow his son's wishes. Jaime's intention was to switch over to engineering soon after admission.

We continued to brainstorm, and Jaime conducted research around Jaime's main passions, including his newly minted, unofficial "nonprofit." He wrote highly intellectual accounts of his activities. Jaime worked quickly to complete his essays by the early restrictive deadline at Stanford. Less than two months later, he was admitted. He wrote me two years later to tell me that he had petitioned the engineering department and gained admission.

The answers are arrived at sometimes through brainstorming and sometimes in a sprint in the weeks before submission, but the answers always do arrive. And through the essays, the evidence of an ability to make a difference in the community shines through. Once a student has identified her particular impact or passion, these powerful essays practically write themselves.

Additional Writings

As many as 80% of college applicants skip the optional essays. Bad idea. I understand how busy everyone is. However, as I remind my students every day, they make a difference. Their pieces don't need to sound like Hemingway. Every piece of writing should serve a specific purpose in alignment with the blueprint or positioning strategy.

Chapter Three

Your Strategy Lands Your Spot

Twenty years ago, U.S. schools were not barraged by applicants from countries around the world. Now, millions of people from every country on the planet seem willing to do almost anything to get their children admitted to a top U.S. school. The rumors you hear are true. Competition is severe.

The good news is that if your child is motivated, he or she can take steps and gain the advantage.

I would estimate that roughly 95% of the general population is continuing to submit applications using strategies that are based on a variety of misconceptions left over from the twentieth century. Students, families, school counselors, and communities continue to operate under a set of admissions rules that no longer apply.

We've all heard that schools once sought the renaissance student. We now know that the idea of the renaissance student is dated. The idea no longer applies. One *could* say that they now want a renaissance *class*, with each student bringing a unique and fiery specialty. What I discovered is that one key point of excellence holds more weight than all the other elements. And that singular specialty is 100% within your child's control.

Schools recruit students solely for their athletic skills; so too, do schools look for students with a point of excellence. In many cases, schools will overlook somewhat weaker grades and test scores in order to recruit students for their talent, ability, or focus.

Generation Z college admissions are an entirely new kind of animal. Yet no one seems to have stopped and analyzed what has changed inside the tight-lipped admissions offices of our nation's top schools. The simple fact is that your child holds within him the ability to focus and take action toward one singular passion and increase the odds of acceptance at top schools two to three times over.

Ignore those who claim he should spend all his free time participating in school activities; ignore those who tell you he doesn't have enough "safety" schools; ignore those who tell you he doesn't have the necessary grades and test scores.

He holds within him the very talents and abilities that are most desirable in today's colleges.

He will simply need to recognize his most unique talent and then create and implement a small-scale project. Once a plan has been developed, most students relish the idea and move quickly to realize their vision.

The writing process is easily directed through a series of brainstorming sessions designed to bring forth the natural intellectual and deep-thinking abilities that most teenagers can access with a mentor or with professional guidance.

From Harvard, I learned that they seek curious and driven students who show a long-shot possibility to go on to start something like Facebook. From Columbia, I learned that they scroll heatedly through the myriad applicants in search of a student who might find a cure for the common cold. From Yale, I learned they are continually focused on landing the next winner of the Nobel Peace Prize or perhaps just your average up-and-coming Meryl Streep.

It may seem like a big hurdle at first, but remember that an effective application is not built in one full-on attack in the month of November of senior year. Rather, it is carefully crafted over the months leading up to application season. The beauty of the thing is shown throughout the process in each small success.

When I started College Prep Consulting as an application development group twenty-two years ago, I hadn't yet joined the admissions teams at Berkeley and Stanford. We knew that 29,000 high schools in America meant 29,000 valedictorians, 29,000 salutatorians, 29,000 student body presidents, and 29,000 editors-in-chief of the school newspaper. We believed we were in the business of helping students to improve their college applications and essays to somehow compete with everyone else. That made sense. That's what everyone was doing…and they still are.

But what I discovered through the years working inside admissions and conducting a dizzying number of interviews with colleagues from Harvard, Yale, Columbia, Penn, and Princeton is that we're not in the application business at all. We are in the positioning business, and we're not just in the positioning business; we're in the *advantage positioning* business.

College List

College-bound students experience tremendous pressure in today's high-stress environment. If left unchecked, this pressure builds and builds throughout the year as app season looms. Our admissions process begins with the initial building of the list of colleges. While this list will likely continue to morph in the coming months, it's a critical conversation starter and point of focus.

Every year, my partner and I begin the process by finding out exactly what makes a student tick.

We want to know as much as possible about the child before beginning to propose and vet colleges and universities. Then we create an overall college list that focuses on a short list of top factors.

I've designed questions to dig deep. Some of my favorites include:

- When you go to the city, do you want to stay overnight, or do you want to get back to the calm of the suburbs?
- What's been your favorite class and why?
- Do you like the size of your school, or would you like a place that's more like a small city?

I love hearing them think about themselves as they grapple with their answers. I myself only applied to one school, and it turned out to be my perfect fit. UCLA was big enough for me to be anonymous. I loved riding my bike from the outskirts of the school, where I lived and worked at the University Co-op, to on-campus classes. My mind was forever filled with ideas, words, and concepts.

I even enjoyed pulling off all-nighters, which included coffee and midnight banter with buddies. My closest friendships began in college, and I cherish that phase of my life more than any other. There is no other time in life when we are so free to spend all our energy to mold our minds and our futures.

The college vetting process begins a lively conversation that spans whatever time is remaining before the month when early applications are due.

This engagement occurs naturally. Students are preparing for the marathon that will culminate in college application season. On one level, they are surprisingly mature—both intellectually and emotionally. On another level, many of them feel like frightened children. Studies have been conducted lately showing that up to 40% of high school girls experience depression and up to 30% of high school boys experience severe anxiety. These feelings are below the surface, and most teenagers don't want to talk about it.

In these cases, it is very important for the child to feel the support of a mentor or friend.

At the same time, the development of the college list often requires some degree of parental involvement. Parents bring a fresh perspective to the conversation while, at the same time, understanding their child's needs and preferences.

In the end, the list will come down to priorities. We draw from a variety of possible factors, and through the process, each student arrives at four or five top factors. The possibilities are endless, but our starting point usually includes the student's planned or possible majors and whether a preprofessional or liberal arts curriculum seems more appropriate. Other factors run the gamut, from such things as structured/unstructured learning environments to accessibility of internships to the availability of subjects of interest—not to mention the all-important social environment.

While my partner and I are very familiar with the top 250 colleges, we are also able to pull from more than 3,500 other schools that might offer the best fit or even the best possible merit aid possibilities.

Selecting Majors

Selection of a major can be one of the most powerful strategic decisions that a student makes in the process.

While some schools receive an overabundance of STEM field applicants, others receive massive numbers of applicants aiming to study other fields. Many students balk at the idea of selecting a box that doesn't necessarily apply to them. They're understandably concerned that they'll be stuck with a major they don't want.

There are schools that make it virtually impossible to switch majors, but they are a dying breed. Most students have no problem switching majors once they have matriculated to any given school. This brings us back to the idea of selecting one's major based upon how well it fits within an overarching strategy.

Still, other schools have departments that are famous and highly coveted. These departments are often nearly impossible to gain access to without an extraordinary point of excellence. And that excellence position must be a near perfect fit. We create strategies to circumvent these challenges.

But it is important to gather all the pertinent information at the earliest possible point.

Some departments are surprisingly small. If a student selects a major that is unusually small, he should know that, depending on his point of excellence, his chances of acceptance at that school may be more limited.

In my work on the admissions team at Berkeley, we were trained to score applicants with a harsh eye if they selected an engineering major. That department is world famous and accepts only forty students per year. I did have a student apply to and get accepted into that department. But…he decided to go to UCLA.

Chapter Four

Applications That Gain the Admit

At both Berkeley and Stanford, our job was designed to decipher the content in the essays. In fact, Berkeley told us specifically to ignore any and all grammar and spelling issues and focus our analyses entirely on leadership, critical thinking, and intellectual abilities.

At Stanford, our job was to decide if we thought a given candidate should be admitted or denied based on a few key factors. But we were only able to advocate to the committee by using words taken directly from essays. We had to decide *yay* or *nay*, and then we had to vigorously cut and paste the written evidence that would justify our vote.

In the fall, when all the other students and families are attempting to throw together a packet of information for the high school counselor, our stealth strategy comes to the fore. The packet your child turns in to the counselor should reflect each element as it comes together to support her advantage position. The guidance we provide to help teachers and counselors write their letters of recommendation is primarily targeted to elicit letters that offer outside support for the student's wholly individual point of excellence.

Another student, Leanne in Northern California, developed her own unique strategy. She was fully aware that there were hundreds of other candidates in her demographic within a hundred-mile radius. She had applied to Stanford her senior year in high school, but she had not been accepted. So, she took a gap year.

Toward the end of her gap year, she found herself continuing to want Stanford, and she began working with our team. We brainstormed ways she might increase her odds, and I told her that she had little chance—unless she could do something that would show evidence of impact.

Leanne was at first taken aback. But after several discussions with my colleague, she had what she later described as an epiphany.

She remembered hearing an account from a classmate who had recently traveled to one of the poorest areas in Appalachia. On the streets of a small town, a young girl had asked her friend for a pen. Apparently, she couldn't attend a local art class without a set of colored pens.

Leanne admitted that she had been awake at night trying to solve problems in her head, and the image of this unknown girl and her need for a pen haunted her. During one pivotal session, she decided to attempt to find a way to get colored pens shipped to this town. My colleague helped her create a to-do list, including who might act as stakeholders and other potential helpers for her project.

Leanne was able to make contact with the group that had led the trip her friend had taken to Appalachia. Leanne then contacted a pen manufacturing company, and soon she was raising small amounts of money through an art supply drive.

She named her cause Pens for Friends. Leanne was accepted to a number of Ivy League and top-tier public schools. But most importantly for her, on this second attempt at applying to Stanford, Leanne was accepted. The difference: a small-scale strategic project, a strategic overall approach, and strategic intellectual writings.

Leanne successfully differentiated herself from every other candidate in her demographic, and exactly one year after having been denied, she received the success she had longed for. She matriculated to Stanford in the fall.

Chapter Five

Standing Out to Get In

Your child's journey toward establishing herself as the impact candidate in her admission pool is precisely how she'll be able to command crucial influence over the committees at top schools and dominate her competition.

The questions we ask through the process are: "Why should committees perk their ears up and listen?" "What might she do to set herself apart from all the other hopefuls in her demographic?"

It's one thing to claim you've started a service project to help mothers in shelters gain access to entry-level jobs; it's quite another to complete this project and also show you know the percentages and the statistics involved in helping a single mother reenter the workforce. The latter will help a student truly stand out.

The Competition

The stronger the connection students build through their activities and essays, the better chance they have to gain admission. Positioning as a change-maker is the cornerstone to generating the emotional element that drives decisions.

How do these students achieve admittance at top schools? How do they position themselves to open those gates and continue opening doors beyond college?

By creating a position and leveraging that position to gain the upper hand among the competition.

By definition, positioning is "a marketing strategy that aims to make a brand and occupy a distinct position, relative to competing brands." Our students excel in a singular area and take the lead.

The Good News

From the early sixties, when admissions committees began to receive greater numbers of applications, they attempted to identify what they wanted in an incoming class. Across the Ivy League and other top-tier schools, they all wanted what were then known as renaissance students. They wanted kids who had done everything from sports to arts to academics.

And this continued up through the nineties. Students began to join as many clubs as they could handle. They became what I call Olympic joiners. And even that wasn't enough, so they fought for the role of president of every club and captain on every team. They aimed for their high school's scholar-athlete award and then fought to take as many AP classes as they could stuff into their schedule. Millions of students are continuing to follow these outdated strategies.

Then, in the late 1990s and early 2000s, these stressed-out, overachieving kids began to be turned away. What?! It was a big shock to everyone. I spoke to parents from an array of affluent to mid-income areas, and I spoke to school counselors, kids, principals, and school boards. Everyone seemed to be shaking their heads in disbelief. Why weren't the top performers being accepted with the same predictability as in the past?

People voiced their frustrations over a system that seemed to have turned its back on all the ambitious kids who had previously walked into sought-after schools. From the outside, this system seemed to have gone belly-up. It had certainly stopped offering a reward for all that hard work.

Soon after this shift, I found myself sitting on the other side of the desk. I was being trained to admit students for entirely new reasons. The admissions world was shifting dramatically, and I was watching it happen.

Colleges were beginning to gain fame not just for winning sports teams; they were noting the fame factor that came as a by-product of students making large-scale societal impact. And then in the same way that top-tier schools recruit athletes in an effort to gain name recognition through winning sports teams, schools from Stanford to Harvard to Yale to Columbia now wanted the recognition that came from being associated with up-and-coming young impact-makers and entrepreneurial good Samaritans.

And it makes sense. Imagine that you are the dean of students at an Ivy League school. Do you want whiz kid test takers and top student club office holders? Or do you want students who will impact your campus and then perhaps go on to impact the world? Most schools would choose to be associated with alumni who are famous for helping to solve global problems.

I attempted to trace this shift back to the turn of the twenty-first century, and in fact the new millennium may have held signs of the shift in its infancy. I believe the shift truly began with the rise of the internet and social media.

But from what I have gleaned, from multiple sources and from other admissions representatives, the shift can be traced most dramatically to the point during and directly after the period of what is now called the great recession.

While transparency from Ivy League admissions is nearly nonexistent, I believe that it is critical that all students are privy to such important information. I believe that people should know what to aim for and how.

The exciting news is that engagement in what we call advantage positioning allows any student to engage in an easy yet powerful step-by-step process that can bump their candidacy up by anywhere between 20% and 80%.

With only a slight degree of engagement and deepened insight as shown in the essays, students can easily gain the advantage.

Overachievers are no longer the most coveted candidates. Even if they were, who among us wants to compete with 29,000 valedictorians, 29,000 salutatorians, 29,000 student body presidents, or 29,000 editors-in-chief of school newspapers? No thanks!

In order to get accepted to his or her dream school, it is imperative for any student to stand out on multiple levels, not just through good grades and test scores. His or her positioning and strategizing efforts, combined with intelligent essays, increase the odds of being accepted at dream schools by somewhere between 20% and 80%. Most students consider it to be worth it.

Using Your Demographic

Advantage positioning is the strategic process of systematically positioning oneself as a leader and expert in alignment with one's passions and interests in one tightly defined area. This small and targeted effort then allows for a natural outsize command and outsize influence over all competitors in the admission pools.

A strategic process requires the creation of a deliberate plan that is executed over a period of time. There is no asking "What do I need to do today?" or "How should I tackle this next month?" Positioning requires the kind of blueprint that can be methodically implemented over several months before submission. No advantage is gained in a sudden, random yanking together of an application under pressure and without deliberate intent.

When you consider the way we achieve success as adults, there are a multitude of similarities to the college preparation process. Every time we set out as entrepreneurs and professionals to achieve anything important, a systematic brainstorming, planning, and organizational process is required—or we know that we are gambling with the outcome.

Yet, our adult processes are the opposite of the typical process of the high school hopeful in his final push through application submissions. Students who engage in advantage positioning and who work strategically and diligently over a period of several months achieve the greatest success. We see this every year.

The advantage positioning process effortlessly mimics the process we use to achieve our goals in the professional arena. But kids come to the process with no prior experience.

Outside of a few highly sophisticated private high schools, the elements of a successful strategic process are never explicitly taught. Instead, kids hit application season like deer caught in headlights, with their hearts hopeful but sadly undereducated about and underprepared for current admissions practices. They've spent four years trying to keep up and stay ahead, and then they are unclear as to how to pull it together and stand out.

Finally, we encounter the last key element in the cycle. The ideal application commands outsize influence over the competition. This is where the advantages of an actual process come into play. A student must position himself in a way that causes college admissions committees to think of him as filling a specific role at their school.

His name should be the first one that comes up when the team gathers to discuss the makeup of the class. For example, if prospective schools trust that he will impact the history department more than other students, he will likely win the admit.

At the end of the day, when a student is competing in the college marketplace for a coveted spot, it's all about the sway that student holds over and above other students in one particular area. This is the crucial element that influences readers and committees.

Entrepreneur Ben Compaine once said, "The marketplace is not a podium in a quiet lecture hall, where everyone gets a turn to speak. It's more like a crowded bazaar in Casablanca. You must distract people from their main occupation—living—and show them that they can't live a minute longer without one of your beautiful rugs."

When your child shows evidence of some sort of specialty that impacts community, he holds a powerful microphone and platform in that crowded bazaar. This makes all the difference.

Positioning, then, is a very systematic, very deliberate plan to gain a position as the expert. Colleges and committees want passionate experts. The student's application becomes a magnet as it attracts a variety of schools. This is in stark contrast to those candidates who must forcefully sell themselves.

The more impact your child makes, the more likely she will reach even further in college and beyond. Once a child experiences the exhilarating feeling of producing herself, she will never go back to following the rules of the pack. The learning curve in the months before application season will propel her into her dream school and beyond.

Case Study: Into Brown

To illuminate another example of advantage positioning, we worked with Marcus, a rising senior in the New York area, over Skype. His mother came to me because he desperately wanted to attend Brown University, but he had virtually no involvement and no volunteer experience whatsoever. His grades and test scores were above average, but his mother worried that his chances were limited.

In speaking with Marcus, we quickly noted that he was a highly experienced break-dancer. Outside of class time, he had spent all of his time break dancing or "breaking." We knew that his mother was right. His chances were slim. But having interviewed admissions professionals across the Ivy League, I felt it was my professional imperative to tell him that he had no chance at Brown—*unless* he made some sort of tangible impact before submitting his application.

Together, we launched into a series of brainstorming sessions to build intellectual essays about breaking. At one point, my partner came right out and asked him if he would consider using all his knowledge to begin work on a documentary about break dancing. Marcus was worried about the time commitment, but we assured him that as he stood, he would not achieve his dream school.

The following week, Marcus and my partner came up with a blueprint, and he was off to the races. Marcus first began to contact prize-winning break-dancers he knew in New York City. He took the train into the city with his friend and used his camera to shoot interviews in a loft in SoHo.

Together with my partner, Marcus discussed how he might capture some sort of intellectual view of break dancing as a cultural movement. He launched into a period of online research and soon realized that the movement was both changing and fading. He decided to focus his essays on the idea that breaking was a fast-disappearing art form. With only weeks remaining before the early deadline to submit his application to Brown, Marcus downloaded editing software, gathered music, shot B-roll around New York with his friend, and wrote thoughtful details about his process.

We also spoke to Marcus about the importance of his letters of recommendation. We helped him to find a way to engage the support of his counselor. Most public schools have a ratio of over three hundred students to each counselor, so it's nearly impossible for any counselor to know what a student has done. But that letter must be written.

We planned the details of Marcus's forms and his conversation with his counselor. We wanted to make sure that she was fully aware of his passion and his project

Marcus likely didn't finish his documentary and he definitely did not show any part of a documentary to Brown. However, his deeply researched and thought-out essays about his efforts to save a disappearing art form combined with his obvious determination to make a real impact were likely the main factors that lead to his acceptance to Brown.

Chapter Six

Seven Pillars
to Yes!

It has been my life's work to help teenagers realize their dreams. In the short time since I served on the Berkeley and Stanford admissions teams, I have developed a powerful seven-pillar system that is helping students gain entrance to their dream colleges.

Pillar One: Letter of Recommendation—
Counselor

Counselors are required to rate each student in a variety of areas. These ratings start at "one of the best this year" and go up to "best in career." Most people aren't aware of this. As we mentor students through these seven pillars, we always start with relationship building. The teacher and counselor letters are a key element to the application, and we do not leave them to chance.

In mentoring kids through a series of mini plans of action through the process, we're able to help students get an early start preparing for discussions with their counselor. We are aiming for a rating of "best in career." What does that mean? We use specific concepts that deliberately encourage recommenders to select the highest rank.

Counselors are awed when they hear about these projects. That awe translates into much higher ratings and much more enthusiastic letters.

Bar none, recommendations are the best way a student can enforce his authority and position and generate the type of buzz that's needed.

Whether a kid claims to be shy or confident, small steps and small actions garner large rewards. Straightforward relationship building cannot be learned too early. These are the things that lead to success in life, and the college applications process is the ideal transition to master these important life skills.

There is some degree of controversy around the question of whether students should seek to sneak a peek at their letters of recommendation. After all, they are allowed by law to see these letters that sometimes determine their fate. Our strong recommendation is to waive the right to see the letters and instead use a series of simple concepts to ensure these key letters are as good as possible. Students should absolutely click the box that waives their rights to see the letters. Colleges aren't stupid. They know that any counselor who has been forced to show their letter will write a different kind of letter. It won't be taken seriously.

While most counselors have a load of several hundred students, there is no better tool to help garner an admission than a powerful letter of recommendation. The ironic thing is that since counselors can't possibly know several hundred students, it's up to the student to tell the counselor what to say in the letter.

Pillar Two: Letters of Recommendation—Teachers

Our goal with teachers' recommendations is simply to deepen the relationship and build rapport. The easiest way to do this is to guide students to drop by and engage with these teachers. Our students prepare for each of these drop-by visits. During their visit, they simply show interest in the subject of the class.

Many students are slow to visit and build rapport because they feel it's too obvious. Perhaps it is obvious on some level. However, there is simply no better way to improve these letters. In some cases, we even have students ask teachers how they can be of assistance in writing the letter. Many teachers actually require this. But we ask our students to offer to supply something in writing.

When given this opportunity, our approach is to ask a student to revisit their notebooks and textbooks to freshen up and share those concepts that fascinated them most in the class. We ask students about in-class performance. Then we encourage them to openly address those areas in which they most excelled or stood out.

Teachers are regularly asked for letters by fifty to one hundred students per year. Writing these letters is a daunting task, especially while juggling a heavy class load of new students. It's crucial that students help their teachers and engage in order to gain the best possible advantage.

We guide each student to follow a systematic follow-up protocol with teachers. These are live relationships in development. Since these letters can have the power to bump a student up into the admit pile, we take them very seriously. All of these actions come together to ensure students beat out the hordes of competitors. A clear best practice is to treat those letters as part of the overall strategy.

We have found that by the beginning of the submission phase, students have become more articulate in their interviews and more forceful and intellectual in their essays. It's a winning combination!

Rachel's Experience

I can illustrate the power of relationships through a story from my own college days. I took a creative writing class at UCLA from a semi-famous writer-turned-professor. He was a sweet old fellow with bushy eyebrows, and he was a fairly good teacher. In my freshman year, I was determined to get straight A's. I instinctively knew that teachers would give me a better grade if I showed extra interest in the subject matter. So, I went to his office hours weekly that semester to discuss writing, and naturally, he gave me an A.

Flash-forward a year, and I took the same class from the same professor. This time, I was busy and less focused on my grades and I neglected to visit him during office hours. My writing had improved, but my grade dropped to a B!

I instruct students to drop by during office hours or during their preparation periods to see if they can engage their teachers in a conversation about their class.

While letters of recommendation are regularly overlooked as a powerful tool, we believe that teachers can be effortlessly inspired to become an advocate, and we explicitly teach our students techniques that help them to ace teacher and counselor recommendations through proactive communications. And once again, these are the same skills that can be used through college and career.

Outside of grades, projects, and personal essays, letters of recommendation are the most powerful element of the application. We work diligently to make sure that the counselor is able to put forth your child as an irreplaceable asset to the community.

These types of additional pieces help the student build her overall presence, or what we call her footprint.

The fact of the matter is that committees trust counselors, teachers, and outside recommenders. Admissions representatives will assume that her point of excellence is truly excellent if there is support from multiple sources.

Positioning is about perception. People buy the perception, and they admit students based on perception.

Pillar Three: Point of Excellence

Now is the time to think far outside the box. What every student and parent should understand is that in the vast majority of cases, positioning does not occur naturally. It does not happen through sheer will. It does not crawl up onto your doorstep. It takes months to create a plan, and just like every other key endeavor in life, it must be deliberately planned and implemented.

A point of excellence, beyond the extra-curricular environment, is the number one most powerful element in any application. Schools have rules and regulations that force our students to jump through hoops, meet deadlines, and fit in with the rest of the masses. These types of efforts simply do not pay off.

The question is, when should you begin to help your child plan and take strategic steps toward his future? If you aim to assist your child in gaining access to a mid- or top-tier school, the answer is *now*.

While we need to allow our teenagers to be the primary brainstorming agents and decision makers, we also need to foster the ability to come up with ideas and solve problems. Now is the ideal time for students to learn to stop, reorient, and consider a shift in direction.

A student could spend several years planning and participating in an array of activities, when out of the blue another student in his demographic could come up with an idea, seek resources, and shoot past him in his applicant pool.

This type of supreme position candidate may seem to have appeared effortlessly and out of nowhere. But we can assure you that this top-of-the-heap position is the product of deliberate actions. It is this type of positioning strategy that allows one student to outflank and distance himself from his competition and gain acceptance at his dream school.

In this highly competitive climate, parents and mentors need to be more proactive in helping each child work toward his potential. The life of the teenager is busier than ever before. We have not seen many students live up to his or her potential without a significant degree of support.

Pillar Four: Teamwork

The best resumes and excellence positions most often do not simply happen on their own—they are often a team effort. We have found that a group effort can make the difference between an application that is perhaps good and strong, to one that pops off the computer screen and forces readers and admissions committees to say "wow" simply with studying, preparing for standardized testing, and engaging in the minimal amount of extracurricular activities. Yet, if the student is aiming high, he or she must think differently and access those adults who will be most eager to help.

You may not realize that your child and family have a network, but we can tell you from experience that every family has a network…and this is crucial.

You may be wondering how to locate a network for your child. Or you may immediately think of someone who may or may not suit the needs of your child's particular excellence project. In our experience, the point of excellence is best designed and developed through some reflection on the availability of resources. Once we begin to land on possible projects with the students, we often find ourselves drawing the parent into discussions. Students are often amazed that their parents can be so useful!

It turns out that the adult world is often the one that is most able to embrace a child through a personal project. We've all been there, and most of us want to be part of the community that mentors and guides a young person.

Sometimes, students need to have their hand held; sometimes, they need help with their approach or their strategy. After all, even though they might be six feet tall, they're still kids.

Think of Mozart. He might not have composed his symphonies had his father not invested time and resources into his lessons. Shirley Temple would not have reached superstardom without substantial encouragement and assistance from her mother. Yet, this type of endeavor should not hinge on the help of parents. Even Shirley Temple became a teenager and, likely, demanded her independence.

Pillar Five: Produce Yourself

If you're depending on your child getting into a top school just going with the flow, we might caution you that this approach may not work out as planned. It is our goal to help you to help your child achieve their goals. This is often the most important point in his or her young life.

The simplest definition of producing that I have found is "to cause a particular result or outcome to come into existence."

A handful of students each year receive perfect scores on their SATs. Understandably, they deserve to feel a bit more relaxed than other applicants; however, achieving a perfect score is never a guarantee to *any* institution and it is certainly no cause for complacency. Times have changed.

Keep in mind that schools no longer troll the pools of applicants in search of stellar test takers. Schools troll for smart kids who will most likely make an impact. Students must "produce" themselves.

When I started a theatrical production company in my twenties, I felt quite lonely and I lacked confidence. I knew that in order to make it in the business, I would need to learn to produce myself. But I felt my youth keenly. I felt like an imposter, and it seemed like everyone would be able to see right through me.

Then I told my friend Pam that I wanted to start producing plays, and she jumped on board. From that moment on, I had a partner, and her addition to the team grew our energy, confidence, and enthusiasm exponentially. Together, we contacted theater owners, actors, and contacts from high and low. Together, we set out each morning to drink hot cocoa and discuss our next move.

While the above example revolves around actual producing in the Hollywood context, it applies to any initiative.

The personal network is key. Using one's personal network is a crucial ingredient in speeding the process and making the widest and deepest progress as quickly as possible. While parents and mentors are great at guiding the student to make some degree of impact, surrounding himself with supportive fellows and friends can be extremely helpful.

I have seen that a good number of our students have difficulty finding responsible teenage partners. Teenagers by their very nature want to be the boss. But there are ways to circumvent power struggles that crop up.

Teenagers are naturally filled with envy, worry, and anxiety. Even when a partner is found, these partners are sometimes lazy, and this too can wreak havoc on one's dreams and plans. Yet, it's worth a try. We help students create workable roles that act as a win-win for everyone involved. We do all this, because when it works, it really works.

The main idea is that even as the project is meaningful and impactful, it should also be fun.

Pillar Six: Whether to Help Your Child

Some parents understandably claim their children should take a more democratic (and independent) route to reach the college of their choice, or they should not get in at all.

We agree.

Yet, we are here to support all students to step forward with their own vision and take ownership in a very specific way that is most aligned with their passions. This effort leads to a fast maturation process that simultaneously builds self-esteem.

We believe that parents can act as the perfect sounding board in this process.

I myself am learning to let my son talk while I sit back and listen. This is not easy at all. I find myself continuing to want to push and shape him at every turn.

Every year, we hear gleeful reports during Christmas from our students who applied through early acceptance programs. Again in the spring we hear the same glee as students receive admits from a wide range of right-fit dream schools. Our work is deeply gratifying from the beginning of the process to the end.

Yet, if one looks at the enrollment of those students entering the most competitive colleges, one will certainly find that these kids have been assisted enormously by families, communities, mentors, or all of the above. A parent is often the best possible partner. Yet, many students will prefer to work with someone outside the family unit.

This is part of the reason colleges must work so hard to locate students from difficult backgrounds and underserved communities; these kids receive an average of 90% less support than their contemporaries and peers from wealthier and more privileged demographics.

We do accept several students each year from underrepresented groups, because we know how exceedingly difficult it is to set oneself apart without tremendous support.

We also understand that many parents in the higher-resourced demographics may be too busy to offer the kind of support that is often necessary to achieve a coveted spot.

This point of view is understandable. We want our kids to learn to navigate their own path. Well-meaning parents regularly send their child to his room to knuckle through the process alone. Some parents say such things as "When he gets tired, bored, panicked or simply worn out from the badgering and stress at the dinner table, the applications will get done."

Some parents believe that if the student isn't up to the task of applying by himself, he won't make it through college anyway. Still others say that they would love to help, but their kids reject any and all assistance.

At one point, my team spent some time surveying student groups matriculating to college. Very few are making it into top-tier schools by working on their applications by themselves. This style of working can be quite confusing. Students working alone or with minimal support say such things as they felt they were living in a vacuum. In addition, their results can be devastating.

Navigating the system these days can be overwhelming. In short, even your competent high school student needs your help.

Pillar Seven: Step In!

A bevy of reasons, including the attitude of most teenagers, cause parents to step far away from this daunting process. In fact, parents cautiously step back in 95% of the households across America. Students and communities often face unfortunate results in the winter and spring of senior year.

While this kind of approach can be comfortable in the months leading up to application season, the results from meta-analyses show that students who face the process alone find themselves attending much less desirable schools, spending several semesters on a poorly chosen major, and often taking five or more years to graduate. Among many other effects, self-esteem can be adversely impacted.

The United States Department of Education has found that students are now transferring schools an average of two times before graduation.

Many of these students are joining the ranks of other students who are returning home in their mid-twenties, because they haven't had luck landing jobs that pay the rent. Much of this can be helped when parents help their child engage with a mentor early in the process.

Parental levels of involvement run the gamut. Some parents drive carpools, attend events, and discuss essay topics with their kids. All of this helps.

Based on what we have seen, it is to the student's advantage to be mentored through junior year in high school and deep into the college admission process. Consider for a moment the traditional words that are uttered by famous people at awards ceremonies. There is usually a long list of supporters that helped that athlete, artist, or star move up through the ranks to the top.

Our advice is to start as early as possible and help your child plan ahead. Simply stated, positioning is an element that can—and should be—manufactured.

Chapter Seven

Future Stars

In the spring of senior year, it's deeply fulfilling to witness a student's excitement as he sees his efforts pay off through the tangible success of the fat white envelopes from long-coveted dream schools.

Your child is a member of Generation Z. Scholars claim this cohort is partly identifiable by anxiety about their future. The impact of this anxiety is seen in unfortunate rises in teen suicide, but it is also seen through the stunning increases of applicants vying for spots in our nation's top schools. Kids long for security.

Gen Z Goes to College

We are experiencing a major shift in the way students apply to college and enter the workplace. The competition for college, internships, and entry-level jobs has increased. One of the effects of this pressure is shown in a measurable drop in self-esteem. Research out of Johns Hopkins University shows student confidence levels dropping by almost 25% in only ten years.

Our Mission: Building Confidence

Every day we hear stories from the parents of our students about the way their child's confidence increased in bounds. While it is extremely difficult to measure confidence in one's child, we all know it when we see it.

Looking beyond this transition, we know that confidence is a key factor to success in life. And there is no better time to build confidence than the college admissions journey.

Is your child capable of engaging in a strategic thinking process? Is your child motivated enough to take steps in the direction of his or her greatest passions?

Just as your young man or young woman is wondering whether success will come, he or she can experience the thrilling satisfaction of a focused and impactful process. Ideally, this process becomes a family affair. Many parents are happy to be able to assist with this type of transition. Other parents have a difficult time merely getting their child to speak to them. I have a teenager too, so I understand!

In the end, our goal is to help our children move easily into a life of purpose and satisfaction.

The life that begins after your child has moved the tassel across his or her college graduation cap is the true launch.

To many of us, a college education can seem like the end goal. But in my personal practice, I have come to believe that the process leading up to application submissions is as valuable as any single part of college. Every year, my group sees students learn to think more deeply about themselves than they ever have before. We have seen them create small projects that reap great rewards. We have seen the thrill of success over and over again. It is truly inspiring.

Many of us reminisce about the days twenty years ago, when everybody applied to one college, got in, and went there. Many of us think today's kids encounter too much stress. We wish it were easier for them.

Having been in this business for over two decades, I can assure you that it is possible to navigate the entire process while remaining nearly stress-free. The process can take your youngster from somewhat driven and somewhat directed to intensely thoughtful and deeply engaged.

Under a thick layer of environmental stress, we find the perfect training ground for life. Through the fine art of dialogue and goal setting, students become drivers of their own destinies. They learn to produce themselves. This period of life is the perfect point to guide a child from reactive student to proactive visionary and change-maker.

Students regularly engage with this process on levels their parents had no idea they were capable of. They switch off the stress and begin to work diligently toward their goals. There is no more inspiring passion than the one that begins to take hold at this time. Exactly at the point when some students are folding inward with stress and worry, others are engaging on the deepest possible level. They all yearn for success.

Some people might wonder if a good college education is worth the level of dedication that is now required. I believe it is. They say that not all diplomas are created equal. Studies show wide gaps in career earnings resulting from different types of diplomas. The biggest earnings gaps are shown in the difference between mid-tier and upper-tier schools.

Our goal is to help kids land their best match school. The experience itself offers all kids an opportunity to expand their minds and engage with a new and changing world. Most of us are hoping to help our youngsters use modern technology as a tool to build a happy and fulfilling life.

The Value of College

Applying to college is now considered one of the three most stressful events in life. Every year, the sheer number of students applying for the same number of seats grows exponentially. Why? Students now understand the degree to which a diploma from a reputable institution can set them up. At the most crucial transition in life, they long for some sort of guarantee that doors will open. While there is no absolute guarantee, there are certainly ways to increase the chances of the best possible results.

In 2008, Berkeley received 42,000 applications for about 7,000 spots. By 2016, competition for the same 7,000 spots increased to over 100,000 applications. The numbers appear daunting. Yet, there is hope.

This book is not simply about gaining admission at an Ivy League school. Yes, to curb the anxiety of your sweet Gen Z child, an Ivy League education would seem ideal. But even a mid-level school offers tremendous value. When you consider name recognition, network, and sheer learning value, mid-tier schools can offer great value.

Of the more than 20 million students attending college in the United States each year, those who attend top schools gain easier access to the top careers; they also rate themselves as enjoying a higher quality of life. We think this is likely due to the fact that they are equipped to accomplish their career and lifestyle aspirations.

The *Digest of Education Statistics* claims that over 20 million students attend college every single year, yet fewer than 1% are accepted at one of the one hundred top public and private institutions. Our message is simply to reach high and protect oneself with options. Whatever the results, we value the effort that was put into the process.

Statistics from the U.S. Department of Education show that graduating from one of the top one hundred schools offers a 90% higher likelihood of a six-figure income by the age of thirty. Some of this advantage stems from the fact that most of those who matriculate to a top school grew up in highly supportive families.

However, a much greater impact comes from the confidence built and the degree of added leverage from a name-brand school. The college alumni networks also extend far into adulthood.

The Advantage

The savvy applicant focuses singularly on gaining a position to potentially answer the committee's area of need. Successful applicants stand out.

You've likely never gone fishing for blue marlin. This half-ton behemoth may be one of the most challenging fish to catch, requiring exactly the right bait.

If I offer you a couple of options for catching a blue marlin, one being an enormous net and the other being the perfect blue marlin bait, which one would you use?

This seems like it would have an obvious answer, but when you relate it to landing a dream school, it's surprising how many students would throw the net. They simply do not know otherwise.

Instead of putting the perfect line in the water with a strategically planned piece of bait designed to hook that exact audience, students are regularly spending their entire high school career preparing their wide net.

And on the other side of the table is a fiercely driven, hyper-focused committee, hell-bent on landing a twenty-first-century kind of applicant. They spend months trolling banks and pools of applicants in search of students they can safely predict will bring the most desirable attributes and qualities to their campus.

To further the analogy, throwing a big, heavy, soaking wet net into the ocean over a long and arduous fishing trip can stress you out and wear you down quite fast, whereas taking specific steps with a keen eye on the line is a more strategic, less stressful, more engaging, and much more successful process.

So, why do students resemble fatigued fishermen throwing their nets over and over again into the murky water? Why aren't they developing just the right bait and strategically positioning themselves so that their target audience can come to them?

Why? Because schools are holding their cards close to their chest. Right or wrong, they are closing the shades as tightly as possible. Students could have no idea how to design their bait and catch their school.

The Magnet Principle

Your child will be attracting her target schools by developing and revealing her singular point of excellence. She won't be casting around aimlessly for whatever happens to be swimming about while simultaneously feeling the stress of a mysterious process with a wholly unknown result. Instead, it will feel almost effortless as she engages her passion and draws better colleges and universities to herself.

This principle goes beyond college and acts as something similar to a rite of passage. She selects her best-fit colleges. Then she takes small steps toward her standout passion. Finally, she picks up speed as she writes strategically to reel in the results. She will achieve her goal. This developmental stage of hypergrowth will lead naturally to a more confident and successful college career and future.

Life is lived best when one is able to set both small and large goals and then systematically take steps to achieve them. There is simply no other skill in life that can impact every area of one's life than the cultivation of the skill of goal achievement. Yet, this skill is never systematically taught. Very few high schools or even colleges teach this crucial skill.

Many of us attend college and then fall into adult life without true direction. As parents, we are still able to guide our kids as they learn to focus and drive their dreams and desires to fruition. The college transition is the ideal launch, as our kids see the direct cause and effect of a conscious and strategic process. Success is within reach.

This is one of the best possible ways we can help our youngsters launch their little boats into the bigger ponds, where they will experience the highest degree of success and happiness.

About the Author

Rachel Collins is an author and speaker who speaks to large and small groups of parents and helps students get into dream colleges. As an admissions reader on the Berkeley and Stanford admissions teams, she makes decisions on thousands of applicants each year. Her program offers an insider's perspective on how to take tangible action and use strategy to hook admissions readers and committees and get accepted. She lives in the San Francisco Bay Area.

A Note from Rachel

There is a continuing and persistent disconnect between what students, parents, and communities believe and what is actually true about how decisions are being made at our nation's top schools. Most people believe that schools continue to operate under the rules of the twenty-first century. But they do not.

Having conducted multiple interviews and led numerous discussions with Ivy League admissions professionals, I can attest to the fact that the rules of the game have changed dramatically.

In addition to conducting my series of interviews at Stanford, my team ventured out and hobnobbed with everyone high and low in the field of admissions. We wanted to know if decisions were being made in the same way across all of our nation's top schools.

The rules have changed. You can take advantage of this change. Please get in touch and let us help you!

Printed in the USA
CPSIA information can be obtained
at www.ICGtesting.com
JSHW080002150824
68134JS00021B/2238